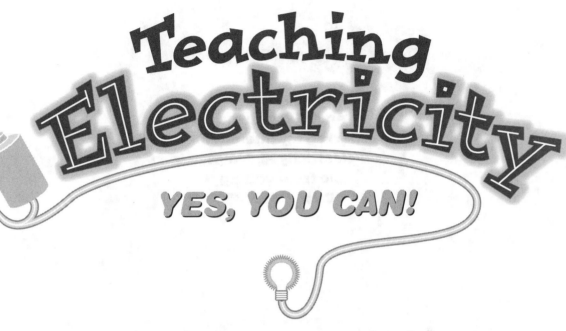

Teaching Electricity

YES, YOU CAN!

by Steve "the Dirtmeister"® Tomecek

SCHOLASTIC PROFESSIONAL BOOKS

New York • Toronto • London • Auckland • Sydney
Mexico City • New Delhi • Hong Kong

Dedication

**To my good buddy,
Andy Fuchs, who
sparked my interest in
electricity and kept
me from getting
"Circuit Bored"!**

Edited by Maria L. Chang
Cover and interior design by Brenda Jackson
Cover art by Rick Stromoski
Interior illustration by Teresa Anderko
with additional artwork by James Graham Hale
ISBN: 0–590–39018–X
Copyright ©1999 by Steve "the Dirtmeister"® Tomecek
All rights reserved.
Printed in the U.S.A.

Contents

Introduction...4

1 Discovering Electricity.............................8
Activity 1: Charge It!.................................9

2 Electrifying Atoms.................................12
Activity 2: All Charged Up!......................13

3 Conductors and Insulators...................16
Activity 3: Go With the Flow.....................17

4 Birth of the Battery...............................20
Activity 4: Turn On the Juice!...................21

5 Electricity and Magnets.......................24
Activity 5: Stuck on Electromagnets.........25

6 Electromagnets at Work.......................28
Activity 6: Got the Message?...................29

7 A Bright Idea.......................................33
Activity 7: Lights On!................................33

8 Socket and Switch 'Em.........................37
Activity 8: Making Connections.................37

9 The Series Circuit.................................40
Activity 9: "Series" Business.....................41

10 The Parallel Circuit.............................44
Activity 10: Side by Side...........................45

Resources..48

Introduction

Imagine for a moment life without electricity—no lights, no stereo, no television, no microwave popcorn! Our world would certainly be a dark and dreary place. Even though we use it every day, and depend on it for so many things, electricity is still a mystery to most people. This book is meant to help solve the mystery of electricity for you and your students by focusing on three basic concepts: what electricity is, how it's made, and how we can control it. The discovery and use of electricity didn't happen overnight, so I've developed a series of activities that loosely follow the chronological order in which different electrical discoveries were made. You'll find that this book paints a basic historical picture of how electricity developed into the versatile power source we use today.

Links With the National Science Education Standards

The study of electricity is a large component of most elementary science curricula, and you'll find that the topics and learning objectives in this book meet the National Science Education Content Standards. Specific points addressed in the book include:

- **Electricity in circuits can produce light and heat.**

- **Electricity can be used to create magnetic effects.**

- **Electric circuits require a complete loop through which an electric current can pass.**

- **Electric circuits provide a means for transferring energy.**

Every activity in this book meets the very first content standard, Science as Inquiry. It's important to realize that science is more than a collection of facts. It is also a process that allows people to draw conclusions about the way the world works. With each activity in this book, students discover for themselves some basic facts about the way electricity works.

While self-discovery is important, we can't lose sight of the fact that there already exists a large body of knowledge in the scientific realm. As both a scientist and classroom teacher, I feel that it's important to give equal emphasis to activities and science content.

In addition to the background information included in the text, you'll find features such as "An Electrifying Fact" and "In a Word," which highlight fascinating science facts and word origins. Use these to spice up the activities and help students see the real-life connections behind the science.

How the Activities Are Organized

The activities in this book are easy to follow and simple to set up, using commonplace materials that you probably have access to either in school or at home. In addition, the activities have been tested in real classroom situations so there should be no surprises when you try them out. For the sake of simplicity, each activity is broken down into the following sections:

Objective a short synopsis of what the activity is all about and what your students will investigate

Introduction background on the activity and how it connects to other activities in the book

Getting Started an opening demonstration that prepares students for the activity they are about to do—without giving away results

Science in Action tips on how to guide student investigations and observations

Questions to Think About critical thinking questions that will help to reinforce the concepts learned in the activity

Science at Home and Science Fair Project Idea activity ideas for students to pursue on their own, ranging from follow-up homework assignments to intriguing ideas for science fair projects

Activity Sheet step-by-step directions on how to conduct the activity, and space for students to record their observations and present their own conclusions. Includes a complete list of all the supplies students need to successfully conduct the activity and wrap-up questions for students to think about.

Management Tips

While the directions for conducting the activities are very simple, it's a good idea to try each activity yourself before doing it with your students. This will allow you to fine-tune the activity to fit the needs of your classroom and will give you an idea of how much time it will take to complete each section. Doing the activity yourself will also allow you to compare your

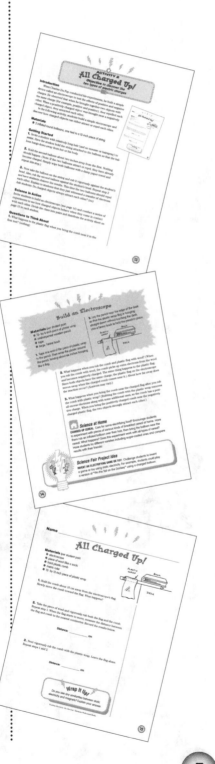

results with those of your students so that you're better prepared to deal with any unexpected answers.

You might want to organize materials in group sets and place them in labeled containers in some central location. This will help you get the supplies into the kids' hands quickly, and it will make cleanup a breeze!

Finally, make sure you allow ample time for your students to complete each activity and plenty of time for questions. Encourage students to share their observations and discoveries with their classmates and to discuss any variables that might have affected the results. Remember that in any scientific experiment there is no wrong answer; there are answers that deviate from the expected result. Figuring out why an answer may be different is as much a learning experience as doing the activity itself!

Sources for Materials

Most of the materials you'll need for the activities are simple and generic. But since this book deals with electricity, you will need some basic electrical components. Supplies like "D" cells (batteries), wires, and flashlight bulbs can be purchased at any hardware or home improvement store. One of the best ways to get materials is to have students bring them in. If you ask each student to bring in one "D" cell or a flashlight bulb, you can usually get enough materials to allow each group to have a working set. To get other items such as magnets and similar supplies, you can contact one of the following sources:

Delta Education: (800) 442-5444
Edmund Scientific: (609) 547-8880
The Magnet Source: (800) 525-3536
Radio Shack: (800) 223-8344
Museum Products: (800) 395-5400
Burt Harrison and Co. (800) MATHSCI

A Note About Safety

All the activities in this book have been tested by students in grades 3 and up. When used properly, the materials are safe for children to handle. Adult supervision is essential when doing the activities with large groups.

The electricity produced by the "D" cells in these investigations is safe for students to work with. Though they may report feeling heat from the cells, the electricity is not strong enough to cause a shock. Make sure students understand that although the electricity in cells is safe to handle, it is very different from other forms of electricity used in school and at home.

Students should also be briefed on how to handle things like glass lightbulbs and pointy wires.

In several activities, specific safety notes are included. Review these with your students before they begin the activity, and everyone is sure to have an electrifying learning experience! Enjoy!

Share These Additional Safety Tips With Your Students:

Using Batteries
- Try to use nonalkaline cells because the alkaline type heats up more quickly.
- If wires become warm, disconnect them.
- Disconnect cells when not in use.
- Don't let students work with cells that have more than 6 volts of electricity.

Using Electricity at Home
- Never put anything metal in an electric outlet or experiment with lamps, electric appliances, or switches.
- Always pull out a cord by its plug.
- Never touch bare wires on a cord.
- Never use an electric appliance near water or with wet hands. Water conducts electricity.

— Steve "the Dirtmeister"® Tomecek

Chapter One

Discovering Electricity

Science Background

To understand how all the conveniences of our modern world use electricity, we must first consider what electricity is. In simplest terms, electricity is energy—the stuff that makes things move! Energy comes in several forms, including heat, light, chemical, nuclear, and mechanical energy. Electricity is special, however, because it's so versatile—it's hard to find devices today that are not powered by electricity. But understanding where this electrical energy comes from has been one of the great mysteries of science.

Electricity is produced by the forces created when tiny electrical particles interact with one another. By controlling these minute "pushes" and "pulls," scientists and engineers have discovered ways of generating enormous amounts of electrical energy using wind, water, steam, chemicals, and even the sun. In order to understand electricity in motion, we must first take a look at electricity at rest: a force known as electrostatics.

Electricity in History

One of the earliest records of electrical experimentation dates back more than 2,600 years to a Greek philosopher named Thales of Miletus. He noticed that after he rubbed a piece of amber (fossilized tree sap) with wool, the amber picked up little pieces of dry grass and feathers. Thales theorized that rubbing amber squeezes out an invisible substance from inside; when the substance rushes back in, it pulls with it attracted particles.

In 1600 an English doctor named William Gilbert repeated many of Thales' experiments using other materials like wax, glass, and sulfur. He discovered that, like amber, many other objects develop an attractive force when rubbed. He named these attractive objects "electrics," based on the Greek word *elektron*, which means "amber."

To test whether objects were "electrics," Gilbert built a piece of lab equipment called a versorium. The original versorium was a thin wire balanced in the middle on the point of a needle so that it could easily turn. Gilbert would rub an object with wool and then hold it near the versorium. If the versorium turned toward it, the object was an "electric."

In a Word

The word *versorium* is a Latin term that literally means "turn about," which is exactly what the versorium was designed to do!

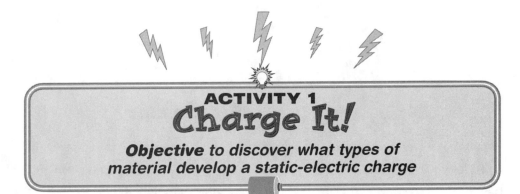

ACTIVITY 1
Charge It!

***Objective** to discover what types of material develop a static-electric charge*

Introduction

When William Gilbert did his experiments in 1600, he used his versorium to test whether an object became "electrified" when rubbed. He discovered that many things were "electric" when rubbed with the proper substance. (We now call this electric energy static electricity.) While he didn't really know why this occurred, his experiments are a good example of how scientists figure out things using experimentation and observation.

In the first activity, students build their own versorium or Static Tester and repeat some of Gilbert's experiments.

Materials

● inflated round balloon
● sheet of newspaper, torn into small bits

Getting Started

1. Put some bits of newspaper on the desk in front of you and invite a student to come forward to assist. (Select a child whose hair has no mousse or hair spray. Chemicals in mousse and hair spray tend to dampen static-electric charges.)

2. Rub the balloon briskly against the student's hair, and then hold the balloon about an inch above the torn paper. What happens? (Some bits of paper will jump up off the desk and stick to the balloon.)

3. Ask students: What force do you think is responsible for making the paper stick? (Undoubtedly, some will know about static.) Inform students that static is a form of electricity that people have known about for thousands of years but have only recently begun to understand.

Science in Action

Divide the class into groups of four. First, have each group build a Static Tester (see page 10). Then distribute the activity sheet on page 11 to each student. Challenge students to find out what types of material they can charge with static electricity.

Questions to Think About

1. Do all the materials demonstrate the same result when rubbed? (no) How are they alike or different? (Answers may vary.)

Build a Static Tester

Materials (per group of four students)
- scissors
- new wooden pencil with sharp point
- 3- by 5-inch index card
- small lump of clay

1. Fold the index card down the middle lengthwise. Cut both ends of the card at an angle so that they make a little point as shown.

2. Place the lump of clay in the middle of a desktop. Stick the pencil's eraser into the clay so that the pencil point sticks straight up.

3. Balance the folded card on the pencil point. Gently blow on the card to test if the pointer swings freely.

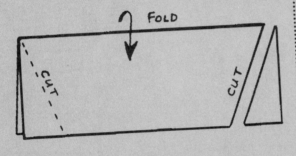

FOLD

CUT

CUT

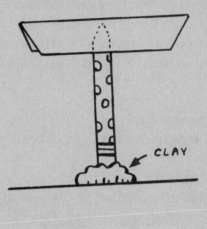

CLAY

2. Are there any similarities between the materials rubbed with plastic wrap and those rubbed with silk? (Plastic objects develop a static charge when rubbed with plastic wrap, and glass objects become charged when rubbed with silk.)

3. Are some materials not charged at all? (Metal objects don't get charged at all.) Why do you think this happens? (Answers may vary. Guide students to the conclusion that static electricity is only generated by certain combinations of materials working together but that some materials just don't seem to work.)

 Science at Home

ALL WET! How does humidity affect static charge? Challenge students to repeat the activity at home using wet objects. Are the results the same? Why or why not? (Wet objects don't work as well because water helps absorb electric charges caused by rubbing. That's why water can help get rid of static cling on clothes and why this activity works best on a cool, dry day!)

Name _____

Charge It!

Materials (per group of four students)
- Static Tester
- 12- by 12-inch piece of clear plastic wrap
- piece of silk fabric
- "test" objects (wooden popsicle stick, plastic straw, plastic comb, metal spoon, metal scissors, glass eyedropper, glass lightbulb)

1. Rub the wooden popsicle stick with the plastic wrap for about 30 seconds.

2. Bring the popsicle stick near one end of the folded card on your Static Tester. Don't let the stick touch the card. What happens to the Static Tester?

3. Record your results on the chart below. Use "strong," "weak," or "none" to describe the Static Tester's motion.

4. Repeat steps 1 to 3 with each of the other test objects.

5. Repeat steps 1 to 4, but this time rub each object with the silk fabric.

Test Item	Plastic Wrap	Silk Fabric
wooden popsicle stick		
plastic straw		
plastic comb		
metal spoon		
metal scissors		
glass eyedropper		
glass lightbulb		

Teaching Electricity: Yes, You Can! Scholastic Professional Books

Wrap It Up!

How do you think a plastic ruler, a wooden pencil, and a drinking glass would react when rubbed with either plastic wrap or silk? Try it and find out!

Chapter Two
Electrifying Atoms

Electricity in History

After Gilbert did his groundbreaking work on static electricity, other scientists continued experimenting with the power of attraction. In the early 1700s, French scientist Charles Francois de Cisternay Du Fay discovered that when two pieces of electrified glass were brought together, they would repel (push away) each other. The same thing happened with two pieces of electrified amber. But when Du Fay tested a piece of electrified amber with electrified glass, he found that the two attracted each other.

After conducting hundreds of tests on different types of materials, Du Fay concluded that there must be two different types of electricity. He wasn't exactly correct. Actually, he discovered the concept of electric charge. To understand how charges work, we have to enter the realm of the atom.

Science Background

An atom is the smallest part of an element that has all its chemical properties. At the core or nucleus of the atom are protons (positively charged particles) and neutrons (particles with no charge). The nucleus carries most of the atom's mass. (Mass is the amount of matter a body contains.) Whizzing at high speeds around the nucleus are tiny electrons (negatively charged particles). Under normal conditions, an atom contains the same number of protons and electrons.

Structure of an Atom

Because electrons occupy an atom's outer edge, they can move freely. Some atoms, like those that make up fur, hair, or plastic wrap, lose their electrons quite easily. Other substances, like rubber and amber, hold on to their electrons tightly and may even grab on to extra electrons from other materials. It's this movement of electrons that creates electricity. Static electricity is the result of electrons moving from one object to another. The electrons accumulate and "stand still" on the second object's surface, hence the name "static."

When you take a plastic comb and rub it against wool, millions of electrons from the wool will cling to the surface of the comb—the comb becomes "charged." Du Fay discovered that there are two types of electrical charges—positive and negative. If an object, like the plastic comb, gains extra electrons, it becomes negatively charged. The wool, on the other hand, loses some of its electrons and now has excess protons. It's positively charged.

An Electrifying Fact
While Charles Du Fay was the first to recognize two types of electric charge, Ben Franklin was the one who labeled these charges "positive" and "negative" after trying many of Du Fay's experiments.

In a Word
In 1805 English scientist John Dalton theorized that all matter was made of a combination of very small particles. He called these mystery particles "atoms" from the Greek word *atomos*, which means "indivisible."

ACTIVITY 2
All Charged Up!
Objective to discover the two types of electric charges

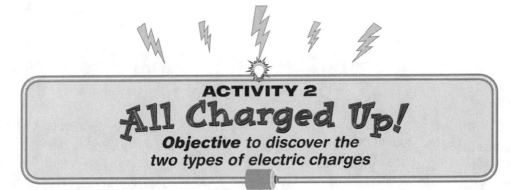

Introduction

When Charles Du Fay conducted his experiments, he built a simple device called an electroscope to test the effects of positive and negative charges. He observed that when he brought together two objects with the same charge (for example, positive and positive), they repelled each other. When a positively charged object was brought near a negatively charged object, they attracted each other.

In the following activity, students build a simple electroscope and discover how charged objects can either attract or repel each other.

Materials
● 2 inflated round balloons, one tied to a 12-inch piece of string

Getting Started

1. Invite a student with relatively long hair (and no mousse or hairspray) to assist. Have the student hold the string attached to the balloon so that the balloon hangs down away from her or his body.

2. Hold the second balloon about two inches away from the first. Nothing should happen. (Note: If the two balloons attract or repel, they have already become charged. Simply wipe both balloons with a damp paper towel and repeat this step.)

3. Now take the balloon on the string and rub it vigorously against the student's head. Also, rub the second balloon against the student's head. Repeat step 2 and have students observe the results. This time the two balloons should repel each other. Explain to students that they just witnessed a transfer of electrons. Ask students: Do charged objects always attract each other? (no)

Science in Action

Invite students to build an electroscope (see page 14) and conduct a series of experiments to see how charged objects behave when they come in contact with each other. Divide the class into pairs and distribute the activity sheet on page 15 to each student.

Questions to Think About

1. What happens to the plastic flag when you bring the comb near it in the first test? (nothing)

Build an Electroscope

Materials (per student pair)
- 12- by 4-inch piece of plastic wrap
- unsharpened wooden pencil
- tape
- large, heavy book

1. Tape one end of the piece of plastic wrap to the pencil. Then wrap the plastic around the pencil, leaving about six inches hanging like a flag.

2. Lay the pencil near the edge of the desk so that the plastic-wrap flag is hanging straight down without touching the desk. Use a heavy book to hold the pencil in place.

2. What happens when you rub the comb and plastic flag with wool? (When you rub the comb with wool, the comb picks up extra electrons from the wool and becomes negatively charged. The same thing happens to the plastic flag. Since both objects have the same charge, the plastic flag on the electroscope moves away when the charged comb comes near it.) About how far away does the reaction occur? (Answers may vary.)

3. What happens when you bring the comb near the charged flag after you rub the comb with plastic wrap? (Rubbing the comb with the plastic wrap removes all excess electrons along with some additional ones, so the comb has a positive charge. When you bring the positively charged comb near the negatively charged plastic flag, the two objects strongly attract each other.)

 ## Science at Home

CHARGED-UP CEREAL Care for some electrifying food? Encourage students to experiment with pieces of various kinds of breakfast cereal at home. Have them rub an inflated balloon over their hair, then bring the balloon near the cereal. What happens? Does this experiment work with all types of cereal? Have students try different varieties including sugar-coated ones and compare results with their friends!

Science Fair Project Idea

INVENT AN ELECTRIFYING GAME OR TOY! Challenge students to invent a game or toy using static electricity. For example, students could play a version of "Pin the Tail on the Donkey" using a charged balloon.

Name _____

All Charged Up!

Materials (per student pair)
- electroscope
- piece of wool (like a sock)
- hard plastic comb
- metric ruler
- 12- by 12-inch piece of plastic wrap

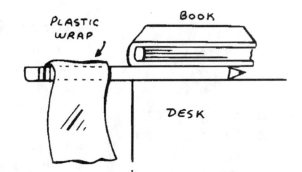

1. Hold the comb about 10 cm away from the electroscope's flag. Slowly move the comb toward the flag. What happens?

2. Take the piece of wool and vigorously rub both the flag and the comb. Repeat step 1. When the flag starts to move, measure the distance between the flag and comb to the nearest centimeter. Record the results below.

Distance: _____ **cm**

3. Next, vigorously rub the comb with the plastic wrap. Leave the flag alone. Repeat steps 1 and 2.

Distance: _____ **cm**

Wrap It Up!
Do you see any similarities between static electricity and magnets? Explain your answer.

Chapter Three
Conductors and Insulators

Electricity in History

By the early 1700s, the study of electricity started to heat up. While Charles Du Fay was experimenting with different types of charges in France, English scientist Stephen Gray made a fascinating discovery. He found that when he brought a charged object near an uncharged one, some of the charge would pass through to the uncharged object, making it attract things too. By experimenting with different materials, Gray found that he could transmit an electric charge over longer distances. The idea of an electrical conductor was born! In conducting his experiments, Stephen Gray found that he could transmit static charge over great distances using metal rods, fresh (green) wood, and even a 700-foot-long piece of thread. Du Fay, in his experiments, went even further. He found that by wetting the thread, he could conduct a charge over $\frac{1}{4}$ mile!

Science Background

In the first activity, students found that things like glass, plastic, and rubber get charged when rubbed. Atoms in these materials hold on to their electrons fairly tightly and require a great deal of energy to move them. When they do move, the electrons usually stay in place until another energy source moves them again. Rubbing a balloon on your head creates friction, which forces the electrons off your hair and onto the balloon's surface. The electrons stay stuck on the balloon. (Remember that static electricity is "standing electrons.")

Most metals, on the other hand, have atoms with "free" electrons, which readily move from one atom to another. When you rub a piece of metal, it starts to get a charge. But rather than staying in place on one end, the charge flows through to the other end. This flow of electrons from one place to another is called current. This conduction of electric current makes the use of electrical energy practical.

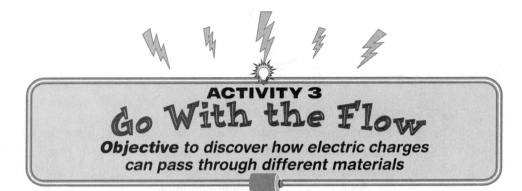

ACTIVITY 3
Go With the Flow
***Objective* to discover how electric charges can pass through different materials**

Introduction

All materials can conduct electricity to some extent, but the differences in their conducting ability can be tremendous. Depending on its type and size, a metal wire can conduct electricity hundreds of trillions of times more efficiently than a piece of glass. Objects like metals, which can carry an electric current, are called conductors. Objects that stop or slow the transmission of electricity are called insulators.

In the next activity, students find out how static charge can be conducted from one object to another.

Materials

- 12-inch piece of insulated wire with the ends stripped
- 12-inch piece of string or twine
- 12-inch piece of plastic lanyard

Getting Started

1. Hold up the string, lanyard, and wire in front of the class. Ask students: Which of these three things do you think would light up a lightbulb when connected to a "D" cell (battery)? Why?

2. After a brief discussion, inform students that in the world of electricity there are two types of materials: Conductors, such as metal objects, let electricity flow through them, whereas insulators, such as string or plastic, stop electricity.

Science in Action

Challenge students to see how well the three different materials conduct electricity. Divide the class into groups of four and distribute the activity sheet on page 19 to each student.

17

Questions to Think About

1. How does the tissue paper react to the different rods when you bring the charged balloon in contact with them? (There's little or no reaction in the tissue paper when the charged balloon is brought near the straw and barbecue skewer. When the balloon is brought near the straightened paper clip, however, the two ends of the tissue paper fly apart.)

2. Based on your observations, which material would work best at transporting electricity from one place to another? (metal) Why? (Metal is a good conductor, whereas plastic and wood are insulators.)

3. Why do the test rods have to be placed across the plastic cup before testing them? (The plastic cup insulates the rods from the desktop.)

TISSUE STRIP

  ## Science at Home

HOMEMADE LIGHTNING Can static electricity light up a fluorescent lightbulb? Invite students to follow these instructions to find out. In a dark room hold a fluorescent lightbulb in one hand at the middle of the tube. Rub an inflated balloon briskly over your hair and slowly bring the charged balloon near one end of the bulb. Students should see a small spark and the bulb should flick on for a second. Have students repeat the experiment, but this time, have them put a piece of black electrical tape over the metal end of the fluorescent tube. What happens? (There is no spark.) Why? (The tape acts as an insulator and prevents the transmission of the electric charge.)

An Electrifying Fact
A bolt of lightning can be six times hotter than the surface of the sun, often heating the air around it to 30,000°C. An average lightning bolt contains between 10 and 100 million volts of electricity!

Name _____

Go With the Flow

Materials (per group of four students)
- 6-inch plastic drinking straw or coffee stirrer
- 6-inch wooden barbecue skewer
- large paper clip, straightened (should measure 6 inches)
- three 10- by $\frac{1}{4}$-inch strips of tissue paper
- 16-oz. plastic cup
- inflated round balloon
- 12- by 12-inch piece of plastic wrap

TISSUE STRIP

1. Lay the drinking straw on the plastic cup as shown. Then hang a tissue paper strip over one end of the straw.

2. Rub the balloon with the plastic wrap to build up a charge.

3. Gently touch the charged balloon to the other end of the straw. What happens to the tissue paper?

4. Repeat steps 2 and 3 at least three more times, observing what happens to the tissue paper. Record your observations on the chart below.

5. Repeat steps 1 to 4 two more times, once testing the barbecue skewer instead of the straw, and then testing the straightened paper clip. Use a different tissue paper strip each time.

Test Material	Test Results		
	Trial 1	Trial 2	Trial 3
Plastic straw			
Wooden barbecue skewer			
Metal paper clip (straightened)			

Wrap It Up!
How well do you think a plastic ruler, metal fork, and wooden pencil would conduct electricity?

Chapter Four
Birth of the Battery

Electricity in History

From the days of Thales in ancient Greece to the mid-1700s, scientists and inventors could experiment with only static electricity. It wasn't until the late 1700s that two Italian scientists, Luigi Galvani and Alessandro Volta, discovered how to produce a continuous flowing current of electricity.

Galvani was a biologist who studied the nervous and muscular systems of animals. One day, Galvani was dissecting a frog on a copper table with a steel scalpel. When he touched the dead frog with his scalpel, its leg kicked. He was so intrigued that he tried to see if he could repeat the action. He noticed that the frog leg kicked only when two dissimilar metals touched it at the same time. Galvani was convinced that he had somehow tapped into electricity within the frog's body. But Alessandro Volta, who learned about the experiment, thought otherwise.

Volta was convinced that the electricity originated from the metals and not the frog. After conducting numerous experiments using different metals and solutions, he had his answer. On March 20, 1800, Volta sent a letter to the Royal Society of London describing his construction of a device known today as the "Voltaic Pile." The first battery was born!

In a Word
The word *volt* defines a unit used to measure the electric potential within a circuit. It is named after Alessandro Volta, the creator of the first electric battery.

An Electrifying Fact
Galvanization is the process in which one type of metal (usually steel) is coated with another type (zinc). This helps prevent corrosion from the passage of electric charges. The process is named for Luigi Galvani because of his discovery.

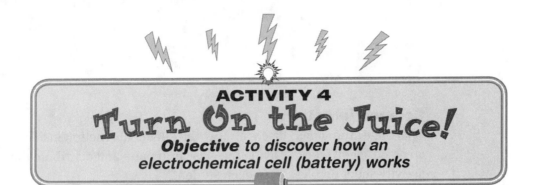

ACTIVITY 4
Turn On the Juice!

Objective *to discover how an*
electrochemical cell (battery) works

Introduction

Galvani's discovery of electricity, misleading though it was, led to the development of the battery. Soon after, new developments in electricity began happening at a shocking pace. For the first time, scientists and inventors could produce on demand a way to store energy that could be converted into an electric current.

While a simple "voltaic cell" is easy to construct, the amount of electricity it produces is so small that detecting it without a sensitive meter can be difficult. By observing changes in two metal electrodes, however, students can see "galvanic action" take place.

In the following activity, students will build a simple voltaic cell and discover what makes an electrochemical cell (battery) work.

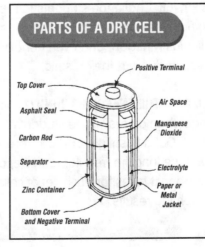

Materials

● a collection of different dry cells including a standard "D" cell (flashlight battery), "AA" cell (pen light battery), 6-volt cell, and others

Getting Started

1. Pass around the different dry cells for the class to examine. Ask students: How are the different dry cells similar? (They all have a (+) and (−) on them, and they all have the letter *v* printed on them.)

2. Ask: Do you know what a dry cell does and how it works? Some may know that a dry cell makes and stores the energy used to produce an electric current and that it contains acid and metal. But they might not be aware of its inner structure.

3. Photocopy and enlarge the diagram of a dry cell for students. Inform them that the first electric cell was invented about 200 years ago by a scientist named Alessandro Volta. Ask: Can you think of anything related to electricity that might come from his name? (The volt, which is what the letter *v* stands for on the dry cell.) Explain that a dry cell works by means of a chemical reaction that goes on inside.

PARTS OF A DRY CELL

Top Cover
Asphalt Seal
Carbon Rod
Separator
Zinc Container
Bottom Cover and Negative Terminal

Positive Terminal
Air Space
Manganese Dioxide
Electrolyte
Paper or Metal Jacket

Zinc-carbon dry cells like this one are often used in flashlights and toys. The electrolyte, a pastelike substance, helps the carbon and zinc become chemically active. When the cell is connected to an external circuit—a wire and bulb, for example—electrons move from the negatively charged zinc container through the circuit to the positively charged carbon rod, forming an electric current. Alkaline dry cells have now become more popular than the zinc-carbon type. These so-called "long life batteries" contain an electrolyte made of an alkaline substance, making them less likely to corrode.

Science in Action

Challenge students to discover how the chemical reaction inside an electric cell works. Divide the class into pairs and distribute the activity sheet on page 23 to each student.

Questions to Think About

1. What happens to the clip and penny after testing it with the dry paper towel? (nothing) Do you think this cell produces electricity? (no) Why? (Answers may vary. For an electrochemical cell to work, electrons have to flow from one metal to another through a conductor—the lemon juice.)

2. What happens to the clip and the penny after testing it with the paper soaked in lemon juice? (After about a minute, the penny begins to get little green spots and the clip becomes tarnished. The longer the "cell" is connected, the more the metals change.)

 An Electrifying Fact

The term *battery* is often misused in science. Technically speaking, a battery is one or more electric cells connected together. A single "D"-sized battery is really a "D" cell. When you hook up two "D" cells inside a flashlight, then you have a battery!

Science Fair Project Idea

CITRUS POWER Challenge students to repeat the experiment using other types of citrus juices (such as grapefruit or orange), acidic liquids (vinegar), and even nonacidic foods (such as potatoes), and report their results.

CAN YOU BEAT THE ENERGIZER BUNNY? Do some dry cells really last longer than others? Invite students to set up a consumer test to find out. Get a flashlight and buy three different types of dry cells: alkaline long life, regular long life, and a generic brand. Test how long it takes for each set of cells to run out of electricity, then graph the results.

Name _____

Turn On the Juice!

Materials (per student pair)
- zinc-plated paper clip (standard Gem clip)
- penny dated before 1980
  (later pennies are not pure copper!)
- 6- by $\frac{1}{4}$-inch foil strip
- 1- by 1-inch paper towel square
- 3-oz. cup about $\frac{1}{4}$ full of lemon juice
- timer or watch with a second hand

1. Take one end of the foil strip and wrap about $\frac{1}{2}$ inch around the paper clip.

FOIL STRIP

2. Place the paper towel square between the penny and the clip. (You'll have a "sandwich" with

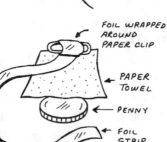

FOIL WRAPPED AROUND PAPER CLIP

← PAPER TOWEL

← PENNY

← FOIL STRIP

the towel in the middle.) Carefully examine the paper clip and penny and record your observations on the chart below.

3. Touch the free end of the foil strip to the face of the penny and hold the sandwich together for one minute. Carefully observe the penny and clip and record any changes below.

4. Now dip the paper towel in the lemon juice and reconstruct the cell as in step 3. Wait one minute and record any changes in the two metals below.

5. Continue observing the cell for two to five minutes longer to see if there are any further changes.

	Penny	Paper Clip
Step 2		
Step 3		
Step 4		
Step 5		

Wrap It Up!

Based on your experiments, can you explain why a cell eventually runs out of electricity?

Chapter Five
Electricity and Magnets

Electricity in History

For a very long time, people had noticed that electricity and magnetism behaved in a similar fashion. But the relationship between the two forces didn't become clear until 1819.

At that time, Danish scientist Hans Christian Oersted was teaching physics. While doing a demonstration for his class one day, he noticed that when the current flowed through a circuit he built, a compass needle on a nearby desk moved. By accident, Oersted found the long-sought link between electricity and magnetism.

For reasons that scientists are still unsure about, electrons flowing through a wire generate a magnetic field around the wire. Coiling the wire around a magnetic object, such as a steel nail, concentrates the magnetic field and transforms the nail into a temporary electromagnet.

Science Background

With the creation of the battery, scientists and inventors finally had a source of energy that could produce an electric current on demand. If you look closely at a dry cell, you'll see that it has two ends—one labeled (+) and the other (−). Batteries and cells produce "DC" or "direct current," which means that electrons flow only in one direction. Electrons exit at the negative end of the cell, labeled (−), the symbol for electrons. A cell produces electricity only when there is a closed loop or pathway that the electrons can follow to get back to the positive end. By hooking up a conductor to both ends of the cell at the same time, you create such a pathway, or circuit.

If you simply take a wire and hook it up to both ends of the cell, you might notice that the wire will get hot. But something else happens as well. As electrons flow from the (−) to the (+) end of the cell through the wire, they produce a magnetic field around the wire. This magnetic field is identical to the magnetic field found around a permanent magnet like the one you have sticking to your refrigerator! The stronger the flow of electrons in the wire, the more powerful the magnetic field becomes.

In a Word
The word *circuit* comes from *circle*, meaning a closed loop that electrons can follow.

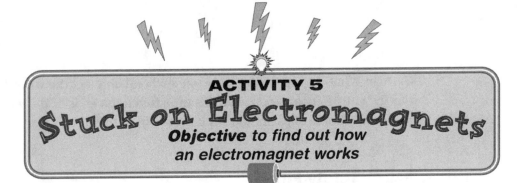

ACTIVITY 5
Stuck on Electromagnets
Objective to find out how an electromagnet works

Introduction

You can find electromagnets in a wide variety of devices, including stereo speakers, computer disk drives, color TVs, and just about anything that has an electric motor in it! Someday electromagnets will replace locks on doors and wheels on trains. They may even launch satellites into space. Electromagnets are so versatile because with the flick of a switch, you can turn them on and off, reverse their polarity, or vary their strength.

In this activity, students will build and test their own electromagnet and discover how it works.

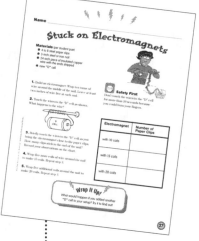

Materials

- 8 to 10 steel paper clips
- steel screwdriver with insulated handle
- 18-inch length of insulated copper wire with the ends stripped bare (available at most hardware stores or an electronics store such as Radio Shack)
- new "D" cell

Getting Started

1. Before beginning the lesson, wrap the wire around the metal shaft of the screwdriver to form a tightly wound coil. Make sure you make at least 20 turns in the wire and leave at least 4 inches of wire free on each end to hook up to the "D" cell.

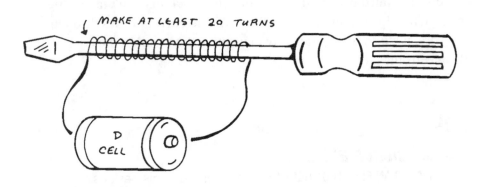

MAKE AT LEAST 20 TURNS

D CELL

2. Place the paper clips in a small pile on the front desk. Without hooking up the wires, take the screwdriver and dip it into the clips. Ask students: What do you think will happen when I lift the screwdriver? (nothing)

3. Ask: What do you think will happen when I connect the wires to the "D" cell? Repeat step 2, but this time touch the ends of the wire to the cell. Some clips should stick to the tip of the screwdriver.

🛑 Safety First

Don't touch the wires to the "D" cell for more than 10 seconds—the cell will get very hot and you could burn your fingers.

4. Disconnect one end of the wire and give the screwdriver a little tap. The clips should fall off. Ask students: How is this type of magnet different from regular magnets? (It works only when electricity goes through it.)

Science in Action

Tell students that they will build their own electromagnet and find out the relationship between the coil's length and the magnet's strength. Divide the class into pairs and distribute the activity sheet on page 27 to each student.

Questions to Think About

1. What happens to the electromagnet's strength as you increase the number of turns in the coil? (The longer the coil, the stronger the magnetic force.)

2. What do you think would happen if you made a magnet with 50 turns of coil? (You'd be able to pick up more clips than with a magnet with 20 turns of coil.)

3. After the third trial, you may notice that the clips don't fall off right away. What do you think causes this? (As the current flows through the wire, it starts to permanently magnetize the metal in the core of the electromagnet.)

 Science at Home

WHAT MAKES AN ELECTROMAGNET? Can other materials besides a steel nail turn into an electromagnet? Encourage students to test other objects to determine their core, such as a wooden pencil, a piece of chalk, a plastic pen, or a brass or aluminum screw. They'll discover that an effective electromagnet needs a core of magnetic material, usually iron or steel.

Name _____

Stuck on Electromagnets

Materials (per student pair)
- 4 to 8 steel paper clips
- 3-inch steel or iron nail
- 24-inch piece of insulated copper wire with the ends stripped
- new "D" cell

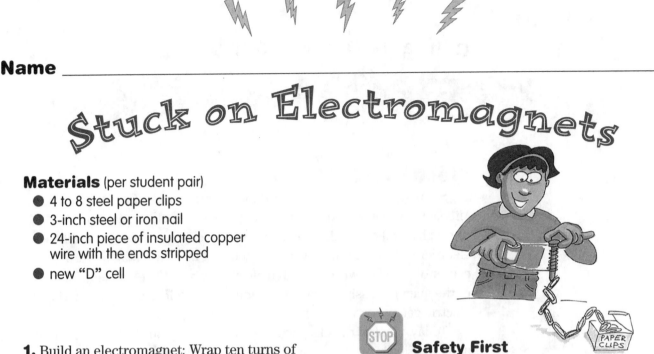

1. Build an electromagnet: Wrap ten turns of wire around the middle of the nail. Leave at least two inches of wire free at each end.

2. Touch the wires to the "D" cell as shown. What happens to the wire?

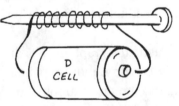

3. Briefly touch the wires to the "D" cell as you bring the electromagnet close to the paper clips. How many clips stick to the end of the nail? Record your observations on the chart.

4. Wrap five more coils of wire around the nail to make 15 coils. Repeat step 3.

5. Wrap five additional coils around the nail to make 20 coils. Repeat step 3.

🛑 **Safety First**

Don't touch the wires to the "D" cell for more than 10 seconds because you could burn your fingers.

Electromagnet	Number of Paper Clips
with 10 coils	
with 15 coils	
with 20 coils	

Wrap It Up!

What would happen if you added another "D" cell to your setup? Try it to find out!

Teaching Electricity: Yes, You Can! Scholastic Professional Books

Chapter Six

Electromagnets at Work

Electricity in History

Soon after Oersted discovered the electromagnet, English scientist Michael Faraday raised an interesting quesion: If electricity flowing through a coil can make a magnet, could a coil and a magnet produce electricity? In 1831 Faraday discovered that moving a magnet through the center of a coil of wire generated electric current. The mechanical motion of the magnet passing through the coil induces electrons to flow. The electric generator was born!

Today, most of the electricity that powers our homes, schools, offices, and factories is produced by electromagnetic generators. In most modern power plants, large turbines—propelled either by high-pressure steam or water—turn the electromagnetic generators.

Back in the 1800s, such generators produced electricity on a much larger scale than in the past and in seemingly unlimited quantities. This helped push the world into the "electrical revolution," driven by the likes of Thomas Edison, George Westinghouse, Nikola Tesla, and Samuel F. B. Morse.

Morse developed the electromagnetic telegraph in 1835 and the Morse code in 1838. Around that time, America was rapidly expanding and sorely felt the need for efficient long-distance communications. It took days if not weeks to deliver messages via railroads, boats, and horseback riders. In 1840 Morse set up a line between Washington, D.C., and Baltimore, Maryland, where he transmitted the first instantaneous long-distance message: "What hath God wrought!" The invention of the telegraph paved the way for the telephone, electronic amplification, speakers, and even the fax!

In a Word

The word *telegraph* comes from the Greek words *tele*, which means "far off," and *graph*, which means "to write." It literally means "to write over a distance."

Science Background

A telegraph is nothing more than a long circuit with an electromagnet at one end. When a telegraph operator wants to send a message, he or she closes the circuit, which turns on the electromagnet. The electromagnet then attracts a steel tab, which clicks. This device, called the sounder, clicks on and off each time the circuit closes and opens. The operator sends a message in the form of dots and dashes by controlling how fast the circuit opens and closes. In Morse code, each letter of the alphabet is represented by its own sequence of dots and dashes. For example, the letter A is •—, B is —•••, and C is —•—•. (See the full code on the Morse Code Conversion Chart, page 32.)

ACTIVITY 6
Got the Message?
Objective to find out how a telegraph sounder works

Introduction

Today we take long-distance communication for granted. We just pick up a phone, punch a few buttons, and *bingo!*— we can speak to someone halfway around the world. While things like satellite links and microchips have improved the speed and quality of communication, the basic concept of instantaneous long-distance communication lies in Samuel Morse's telegraph system.

In this activity, students will build their own electromagnetic telegraph and send each other messages.

Materials

● ruler

Getting Started

1. Have the class sit quietly. Tell students that you are going to send them a secret message that they have to decode.

2. Using a ruler, make three very fast taps followed by three slow taps then three very fast taps on the desk. Ask: Who knows what the message is? (Some students might recognize the pattern as ●●● ▬ ▬ ▬ ●●●, or SOS.) Explain to students that SOS was chosen as the universal distress signal in Morse code because this combination of letters creates an a distinct and unmistakable sound pattern. The Morse code is a way of sending messages over long distances using a device called the telegraph.

Science in Action

Divide the class into groups of four. Tell students that they will build a simple Telegraph Tapper (see page 30) and then send a message to other members of their group. Distribute the activity sheet on page 31 and the Morse Code Conversion Chart on page 32 to each student.

Questions to Think About

1. Why do you need to have at least 40 turns of wire on the nail to make the sounder work? (You need a strong magnetic field to pull the nail head and thumbtack together.)

2. Could a brass paper fastener replace the steel thumbtack in the sounder? (no) Why? (Brass is not magnetic.)

Build a Telegraph Tapper

Materials (per group of four students)
- 3-inch steel nail
- fist-sized lump of clay
- 20-inch-long piece of thin, insulated wire, with ends stripped bare (available at a hardware store or electronics store such as Radio Shack)
- 5- by 1-inch strip of index card
- steel thumbtack
- 3 or 4 large books or wooden building blocks
- "D" cell
- tape

1. Wrap at least 40 turns of wire around the middle of the nail to form the electromagnet. Make sure to leave at least 5 inches of wire on each end of the coil to attach to the "D" cell.

2. Push the thumbtack through the middle of the index card strip, about $\frac{1}{4}$ inch from one end.

3. Set up your telegraph sounder as shown. Make sure the nail rests directly under the thumbtack. The gap between the two should be about $\frac{1}{8}$ inch.

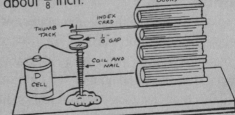

4. Securely tape one end of the wire coiled around the nail to the flat end of the "D" cell. Briefly touch the other end of the wire to the bumpy end of the cell. The electromagnet will attract the thumbtack and make a "click." Lift the wire and the thumbtack should release. (If the thumbtack stays stuck to the nail, the gap between the two is too small. Adjust the nail in the clay to add more space between the two. If the thumbtack doesn't stick to the nail, the gap is too wide.)

3. Why do you need to adjust the position of the nail head before sending your messages? (To get the clicking sound, you need to have a significant distance between the nail head and the thumbtack.)

 Safety First

Tell students not to touch the "D" cell for more than 10 seconds at a time because they could burn their fingers.

Science Fair Project Idea

LONG-DISTANCE TAPPING The real test of any communication device is to send messages over a distance! Challenge students to build a system that would work between rooms at a distance of more than 20 feet. (Students may need to use a 6-volt lantern battery instead of the "D" cell.)

Got the Message?

WHO NEEDS E-MaiL!

Materials (per group of 4 students)
- Telegraph Tapper
- Morse Code Conversion Chart
  (from your teacher)

1. Write a simple one-line message below.

Safety First
Don't touch
the wire to the
"D" cell for more
than 10 seconds
at a time because
you could burn
your fingers.

2. Use your Morse Code Conversion Chart to translate your message into Morse code, or dots and dashes.

3. Send your message on the Telegraph Tapper. Pause at least one second between letters and three seconds between words. Other members of your group will record the Morse code and translate it.

Wrap It Up!

Compare the Morse code message that you sent to the message that your group recorded. How similar are they? Can you think of any reason why there might have been differences?

4. Now record the Morse code message your friend sent below.

5. Use the chart to convert the code back to English.

Morse Code
Conversion Chart

A	•—		T	—
B	—•••		U	••—
C	—•—•		V	•••—
D	—••		W	•——
E	•		X	—••—
F	••—•		Y	—•——
G	——•		Z	——••
H	••••			
I	••			
J	•———		1	•————
K	—•—		2	••———
L	•—••		3	•••——
M	——		4	••••—
N	—•		5	•••••
O	———		6	—••••
P	•——•		7	——•••
Q	——•—		8	———••
R	•—•		9	————•
S	•••		0	—————

Chapter Seven
A Bright Idea

Electricity in History

Most people know that Thomas Edison invented the first practical lightbulb. But the process behind his invention dates back thousands of years. For a long time, people had known that heating certain materials, like iron in a fire, makes them glow. This process, called incandescence, doesn't produce a great deal of light when the object is heated from the outside. But what would happen if you heated the object from the inside?

Edison knew that an electric current running through a wire makes the wire glow red hot. And when the wire is very thin, it burns white hot for a few seconds before melting. Edison put a thin wire inside a glass bulb and developed the filament.

The next step was to find the right material for the filament—something that would glow long enough to produce a decent source of light. Early experiments with the element carbon proved to be a bust. Carbon would burn up, or combust, long before it glowed. That's because air would leak into the bulb and oxygen would make the carbon burn.

Finally, Edison's chief assistant Charles Batchelor decided to try a vacuum bulb— a bulb that had virtually no air inside. He fashioned a filament out of carbonized silk thread and the bulb lit up! The first bulb, which was created on October 21, 1879, lasted more than 40 hours.

An Electrifying Fact
To see incandescence in action, take a look inside a toaster oven when it's on. As electricity flows through the wire coils, they begin to glow red hot.

ACTIVITY 7
Lights On!
Objective to discover how an electric light works

Introduction

Today you can find electric lights of virtually every design and brightness. Although these lights may all seem different, there are really only two forms in use. Fluorescent lights (the long glass tubes) contain a kind of gas that glows when electricity passes through the tube. Incandescent lights (the kind found in most homes, lamps, and flashlights) use electricity to heat up a filament. The filament is usually made from a tungsten alloy. When the filament gets hot enough—reaching almost 3,000°C—it glows, without melting.

For a lightbulb to work, electricity has to pass through the filament

and return to the power source to complete the circuit. Like a dry cell, a lightbulb has two ends, but they sit next to each other. Look closely at the bottom of a lightbulb. You'll see a small silver tip. This is a solder connection between one end of the filament and the outside of the bulb. A second solder at the screw part of the bulb connects to the other end of the filament. The black ring at the bottom of the bulb keeps the two ends of the bulb from touching. To light the bulb, both ends of the bulb have to connect to the two ends of a dry cell with a wire. Once the circuit is complete, the bulb will light.

In the following activity, students will build a simple flashlight to discover how an electric light works. Challenge them to come up with different ways to complete a simple circuit.

Materials
● desk lamp with a large, clear-glass lightbulb

Getting Started
1. Have students observe the desk lamp in the front of the room and turn it on. Ask a volunteer to describe what's going on inside the bulb to make it light. (Electricity goes through the little wire, or filament, in the bulb and makes it so hot that it glows.)

2. Turn off and unplug the lamp. Unscrew the bulb and walk around the room. Have the class examine the bulb closely. Explain to students that for the bulb to light, electricity has to get in one end and out the other.

Science in Action
Invite students to build a simple flashlight using a flashlight bulb, a "D" cell, and a strip of aluminum foil.* (See instructions below.) Their mission is to find how many different ways they can connect the bulb and "D" cell to get the bulb to light. Divide the class into pairs and distribute the activity sheet on page 36 to each student.

How to make foil strips: Lay out about 3 feet of foil, dull side up. Lay the edge of a ruler about 1 inch in from the edge of the foil. Pull up on the foil so that it tears against the edge of the ruler. Fold each strip in half lengthwise. Repeat until you have enough strips for each student pair. Some of the activities in this book call for 6- by $\frac{1}{2}$-inch strips. Simply cut the 12-inch strips in half.

* Note: For activities 7 through 10, instead of foil strips you can use pieces of insulated wire with $\frac{1}{2}$ inch stripped bare at the ends. Simply cut them to size (12 or 6 inches, depending on the activity).

Questions to Think About

1. Why must you hook up both ends of the "D" cell to two contact points on the bulb (the metal collar and the bottom) to get a successful circuit? (For a lightbulb to work, electricity must flow through the bulb and back into the cell.)

2. What part of the bulb must touch the foil strip and the cell? (The metal conducting parts of the bulb must touch the foil strip and the cell's contacts so the current can flow through.)

3. Does it matter which direction the cell faces to get the bulb to light? (The bulb will work no matter which way the cell is facing.) What does this tell you about the way a lightbulb functions? (As long as the circuit is complete, the bulb will light regardless of which direction the current flows.)

Four Ways to Light the Bulb

1 2 3 4

 ## Science at Home

KOOKY CONDUCTOR TESTER Using the simple circuit setup shown here, students can test to see which other materials conduct electricity well. Tape one end of a foil strip to the flat end of a dry cell. Wrap one end of the other strip around a flashlight bulb. Use a clothespin to hold the strip in place. Use the clothespin to touch the bulb to the dry cell. Then place objects like a penny, a metal spoon, a paper clip, a brass fastener, a piece of Mylar, a piece of fruit, fake fur, or other materials between the loose ends of the strips. The brighter the bulb lights, the better the object is at conducting electricity!

Science Fair Project Idea

BRIGHT ANSWERS Challenge students to use a simple circuit (dry cell, foil strips, and flashlight bulb) to create a game board or quiz master to "flash" correct answers. (For these games to work, students will need to figure out a way to insulate any foil strips that overlap. Without insulation, any combination of overlapping strips will light the bulb. A simple method is to apply strips of masking tape to one side of the foil strips, leaving some foil exposed at each end.

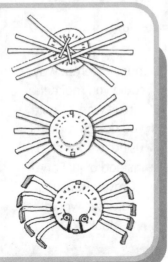

Lights On!

Materials (per pair of students)
- "D" cell
- 12- by $\frac{1}{2}$-inch foil strip
- flashlight bulb

1. Using the materials above, see how many ways you can connect them to get the bulb to light. (Hint: Remember that a circuit is a complete loop that electricity can flow through.)

2. Each time you get the bulb to light, draw the circuit below.

Circuit A:

Circuit B:

Circuit C:

Circuit D:

Wrap It Up!

Based on your experiment, how many different ways could you make the circuit work? Could you design a circuit using two foil strips instead of just one? Draw what such a circuit would look like.

Chapter Eight
Socket and Switch 'Em

Electricity in History

After Edison and his associates perfected the lightbulb, their work just got harder. Not only did they have to set up a plant to manufacture the bulbs, they also had to design a system for large-scale power generation and distribution. For the electric light to become an everyday convenience, there had to be a central distribution system from which power lines could run to each and every house, factory, and office. In September 1882 Edison opened the first permanent commercial power plant on Pearl Street in New York City.

In the early days of electric lights, all the connections between the wiring system and the bulbs were "hard wired." This meant that every time a bulb blew out, an electrical technician had to change it! Edison knew that to sell bulbs, he would have to make them cheap, disposable, and easy to change. So he and his staff set about creating a "universal connector," which anyone could operate.

One of the people assigned to the task was an African American scientist named Lewis Latimer, an expert draftsman and designer. To be effective, a connector had to hold a lightbulb firmly in place and provide electrical contacts to both ends of the bulb. After much experimenting, Latimer came up with a device that is similar to the screw-in connector we use today.

ACTIVITY 8
Making Connections
Objective *to discover how sockets and switches work*

Introduction

Imagine what it would be like if you had no light switch to turn on a bulb when you walk into a room. First, you would have to find the wires running from the power source to the bulb. (That can be tricky business in the dark!) Then, holding the wire by the insulation (so that you don't accidently electrocute yourself), you would have to touch it against one of the bulb's terminals to complete the circuit.

A light switch opens and closes the circuit without having to disconnect any wires. Think of the switch as a drawbridge for electricity: When the bridge is up, electrons can't get through!

In the following activity, students will build a flashlight using a socket and switch made from common household materials.

Materials
- flashlight with a switch
- "D" cell
- foil strip (see page 34)
- flashlight bulb

Getting Started

1. Ask for a volunteer to come forward and assemble a simple flashlight like the one in activity 7.

2. While the student is holding the simple circuit, take out the flashlight with the switch. Turn the flashlight on and off several times. Ask students: Which flashlight would they prefer to have?

3. Tell students that while both lights do the same job, the assembled flashlight is more convenient because all of the connections are together inside. The flashlight has a socket to hold the bulb and a switch to turn it on and off.

Science in Action

Tell students that their mission is to build a flashlight using a homemade switch and socket. Pair off students and distribute the activity sheet on page 39 to each student.

Questions to Think About

1. Why do you need to put tape over the ends of each paper fastener? (The tape acts as an insulator between the connections.)

2. Why should the brass fasteners not touch each other along the bottom of the switch? (If the ends of the fasteners touch each other, you will get a "short circuit" and electricity will not flow along the desired path.)

3. Why must you use brass and steel fasteners to make your socket? (Brass and steel conduct electricity.) Would a plastic or painted paper clip work? (no) Why? (Plastic and paint act as insulators and will block the flow of electrons.)

Science Fair Project Idea

DESIGN A BETTER SOCKET In activity 8 students build a basic socket, but more improvements can be made. Challenge students to assemble their own socket-and-switch system using materials found around their home. Have them report their results and show samples of their work.

Name _____

Making Connections

Materials (per student pair)

- "D" cell
- three 6- by $\frac{1}{2}$-inch foil strips
- flashlight bulb
- spring-type clothespin
- rubber band
- 8- by 10-inch piece of cardboard
- 2 brass paper fasteners
- steel paper clip
- tape
- hole punch

1. Wrap one foil strip around the bulb's base. Use the clothespin to hold the strip and the bulb in place. Tape another foil strip to the bottom of the bulb. Be sure that the foil makes contact with the bulb. This setup is your socket.

2. Double-wrap a rubber band around the "D" cell, then tape it in place as shown. Slip the end of the foil strip attached to the socket under the rubber band at one end of the "D" cell. Insert one end of the second foil strip under the rubber band at the other end of the cell. Then tape the cell to the cardboard.

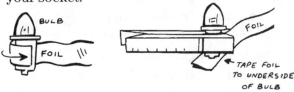

3. Punch a hole near the free ends of the foil strips. Put the fasteners through the holes in the strips. Then push the fasteners through the cardboard. Make sure the distance between the fasteners is slightly less than the length of a paper clip. Open the ends of the fasteners underneath the cardboard. Make sure they don't touch each other, and tape the ends in place.

4. Slip a paper clip around the head of one of the fasteners as shown. The clip should fit snugly but move back and forth easily. The switch is now complete.

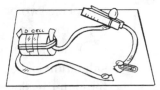

5. Slide the paper clip on the switch so that it bridges the gap between the two fasteners. The bulb should light! You control the circuit by sliding the paper clip on and off the fastener.

Wrap It Up!

What would happen if you replaced the steel paper clip with a plastic-coated paper clip?

Chapter Nine

The Series Circuit

Electricity in History

In the early days of electrical power, almost all the telegraph lines were wired in large series circuits, which sometimes stretched over hundreds of miles. In a series circuit, many different components are all connected in a row or "series" with only one path for electrons to follow. Because there was only one path, any break in the wire along the way meant that the messages were stopped. It didn't take long before clever train robbers learned that they just needed to cut the telegraph line in one place, and they would be able to attack a train and get away scot free. Messages sent to intercept the robbers were stopped dead in the line!

Science Background

In a series circuit, there is only one pathway for electricity to go. A break in the circuit disrupts the current flow. If you've ever worked with strings of holiday lights, you've probably experienced the frustration of having all the lights go out when a single bulb blows. You have to check each bulb to restore the flow of electrons.

Series circuits that require more than one cell also present another problem. If you place cells in the wrong direction, the device won't work. That's because electrons flow through a cell in only one direction. When you place two or more cells in series, the (+) of one cell connects to the (−) of the next.

When a series circuit contains several components, an important consideration is the amount of electricity flowing through the circuit. Two different terms describe how much electricity flows from one place to another. Voltage measures the amount of electrical pressure or "push." Current measures the total amount of electricity flowing past a given point. A simple way to look at the flow of electricity in a circuit is to compare it to water flowing in a pipe. Total current (measured in amps) would be how much water is flowing in the pipe, while voltage (measured in volts) is the pressure pushing the water along. In the United States, the voltage of normal household current is set at either 110 or 220 volts. The current, on the other hand, depends on how many appliances are being used. The more appliances used, the greater the amperage (the current's strength).

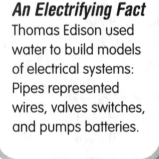

An Electrifying Fact

Thomas Edison used water to build models of electrical systems: Pipes represented wires, valves switches, and pumps batteries.

In a Word

The series circuit gets its name from the fact that all the components follow each other in a single row—just as the World Series is a bunch of games played in a row!

ACTIVITY 9
"Series" Business
Objective to discover how a series circuit works

Introduction

You can change the amount of electricity flowing through a series circuit by changing the number of cells or the amount of "load." The load is the number of objects using electricity and could range from lightbulbs to buzzers to light-emitting diodes (LEDs).

In the following activity, students will discover what happens in a series circuit when they change the voltage and the load by adding and subtracting cells and bulbs. Students will use the sockets and switches they constructed in activity 8.

Materials
● 8 to 10 dominoes

Getting Started

1. Place the dominoes on the desk in front of the room so everyone can see them. Set up the dominoes on end close enough so that when one falls, it will start a chain reaction and the rest will also fall.

2. Invite a volunteer to come up and knock over the end domino.

3. Set up the dominoes exactly as before, but this time remove two from the middle. Ask students: What will happen when one end is knocked over again? Get another volunteer to knock over one end. The dominoes will fall until they reach the break in the sequence.

4. Explain to students that the line of dominoes is similar to a series circuit in electricity. In a series circuit, each component directly follows the one before. If there is a break at any point in the circuit, the electricity stops and the entire circuit goes dead.

Science in Action

Invite students to test the behavior of a series circuit using a combination of different sockets, switches, and cells. Refer back to activity 8 for detailed instructions on how to build the socket and switch. Pair off students and distribute the activity sheet on page 43 to each student.

Questions to Think About

1. How do you have to connect the two "D" cells in order to get the bulb to light? (The cells have to be aligned so that the (+) of one is connected to the (–) of the next. This is because electrons flow in a cell in only one direction.)

2. What happens to the bulb's light when you add a second "D" cell? (The bulb gets brighter.) Why? (The voltage of the second cell was added to the first. An increase in voltage translates to an increase in brightness.)

3. What happens to the first bulb's light when you add a second bulb to the circuit? (The first bulb grew dimmer.) Why? (The electricity has to pass through two filaments in a row. The load is additive, meaning the more bulbs in a circuit, the dimmer their light.)

4. Does it matter where in the circuit you connect the second bulb? (no) Why? (The second bulb will still be part of one circuit.)

5. Why do both lights go off when you turn off the switch? (There is only one circuit through which electricity passes.)

Series Circuit With Two "D" Cells

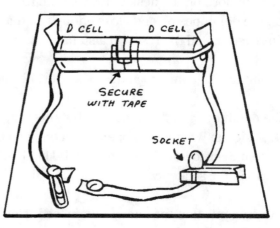

Series Circuit With Two "D" Cells and Two Bulbs

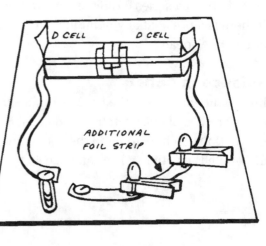

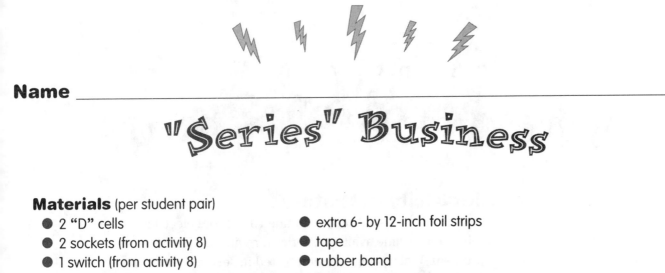

Name _____

"Series" Business

Materials (per student pair)
- 2 "D" cells
- 2 sockets (from activity 8)
- 1 switch (from activity 8)
- extra 6- by 12-inch foil strips
- tape
- rubber band

1. Construct a basic circuit using a bulb, "D" cell, socket, and switch. Test the circuit to make sure it works. This will be the "control" against which you will compare other circuits you will build. Draw a diagram of your basic circuit.

2. Add a second "D" cell to the first one. Use tape and a rubber band to connect both cells. Can you get the circuit to light? Draw a diagram of the new circuit showing how the cells are aligned. Record any changes in the bulb's behavior.

3. Add another socket, bulb, and foil strip to the circuit in step 2. Can you get the second bulb to light? Draw a diagram of the new circuit and record your observations. Turn the switch on and off several times to see what happens to the two bulbs.

Wrap It Up!

If all the lightbulbs in your home were connected with a series circuit, what would happen when you turned off a light switch? Why?

Teaching Electricity: Yes, You Can! Scholastic Professional Books

Chapter Ten
The Parallel Circuit

Electricity in History

As the use of electricity expanded and more electric appliances became available, series circuits quickly became a problem. When things are connected in series, their load or resistance adds up, which often results in burning wires. In addition, if there is only one break in the circuit, all the components shut down. The need for an alternative system of wiring was obvious, and the parallel circuit was born.

In modern times, parallel circuits are the safest way to go, but in the early days of power production, things often got a bit wild. Back in 1882, Thomas Edison himself experienced a near disaster with the first central power plant constructed for commercial use at Pearl Street in New York City. Like today, most power lines running from the station ran underground and were wired in parallel circuits that met at large junction boxes under the street. One day, a policeman came running into the station to tell Edison to shut off all the power. It seemed that one of the junction boxes wasn't wired correctly and was leaking electricity into the surrounding wet soil. The leak was discovered by a poor old horse who was pulling a beat-up junk wagon. When the horse stepped on the road above the junction box, he got the shock of his life. He reared straight up in the air and ran wildly down the street, knocking over pushcarts and pedestrians and dragging the junk man behind him.

In a Word
The word *parallel* means two objects run side by side without ever intersecting. A good example would be the two rails on a railroad track. They run side by side over great distances but never cross except at switches.

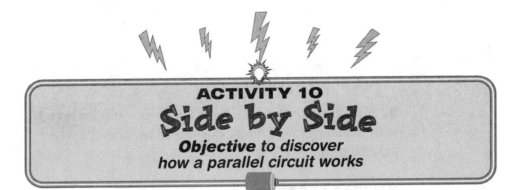

ACTIVITY 10
Side by Side
***Objective** to discover
how a parallel circuit works*

Introduction

As you might have guessed, in a parallel circuit, two sets of wires run side by side off a common power supply. This way, devices installed on one circuit won't interfere with devices connected on another.

Parallel circuits offer much greater convenience and flexibility than series circuits. They also offer an additional benefit when it comes to carrying a load. In a series circuit, as you add more components, the load increases. In a parallel circuit, the loads are split on different lines. A lightbulb, for example, always burns at its maximum brightness, limited only by the total available current.

You've probably noticed that if you turn off a light switch in a room, only one or two lights are affected. But if you "blow a fuse," they all go out. In most cases, all the lights in a given room are wired in parallel off a common power supply. When the fuse blows, the power supply itself shuts down.

In the final activity, students will build a parallel circuit and compare its efficiency to a series circuit. As in the previous activity, students will use the sockets and switches that they built in activity 8.

Materials

● classroom lights, if they have more than one switch
(or two desk lamps each plugged into the same electric outlet)

Getting Started

1. Have the class direct their attention to the room lights. Invite a volunteer to come up and turn off one of the light switches. (Note: If you only have one light switch for the room light, set up two desk lamps plugged into the same electric outlet. Then have the volunteer turn off only one switch.) Have students observe what happens. (Some of the lights will stay on even though the switch is off.)

2. Ask students: Based on what you learned in the previous activity, do you think the lights in the room are wired in a series circuit? (no) Why? (Some of the lights stay on when the switch is turned off. If it were a series circuit, all of the lights would go off!)

3. Explain to students that most buildings today are wired with "parallel circuits." Ask students: What does the word *parallel* mean?

Science in Action

Challenge students to use a combination of sockets, switches, and "D" cells to build and test the behavior of a parallel circuit. (Refer back to activity 8 for detailed instructions on how to make the basic socket and switch. For this activity, students may find it easier to assemble both switches on one piece of cardboard.) Pair off students and distribute the activity sheet on page 47 to each student.

Questions to Think About

1. In the first test circuit, what happens to the two bulbs when you turn on only one switch? (Only one bulb turns on.) Why?

2. How is the behavior of the parallel circuit different from the series circuit? (In a parallel circuit, each switch controls a different bulb.)

3. How does the bulbs' light with the two cells wired in series compare to the bulbs' light when you connect the two cells in parallel? (When the two "D" cells are connected in parallel, both bulbs are dimmer than when the cells are wired in series.) Why does this happen? (The voltage produced by the two cells wired in parallel is not added together. Instead, the total voltage is equal to the voltage of only one "D" cell. But the total amount of electric current has doubled.)

Science Fair Project Idea

A MODEL HOME Challenge students to build a model of the electrical system in their home. They can start by connecting two or three "D" cells in a series. Then, using the sockets and switches from activity 8, construct several parallel circuits that cover different rooms.

Name _____

Side by Side

Materials (per student pair)
- 2 "D" cells
- 2 sockets (from activity 8)
- 2 switches (from activity 8)
- extra 6- by $\frac{1}{2}$-inch foil strips
- rubber band

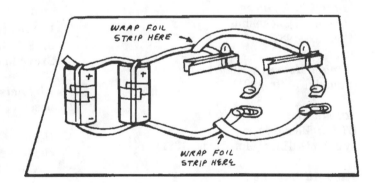

1. Build the basic test circuit as shown. (Note that the bulbs are parallel but the "D" cells are in a series.)

2. Test the circuit by turning on one switch, and then the other. In the space below, record any changes in the two bulbs.

3. Reconnect the two "D" cells so that they are also in parallel as shown. Turn the switches on and off, and record your observations about the bulbs.

Wrap It Up!

Which parallel circuit produced brighter light?
Why do you think that is?

Teaching Electricity: Yes, You Can! Scholastic Professional Books

Resources

Books

Dear Mr. Henshaw by Beverly Clearly
(Dell, 1983)

Electricity by Steve Parker
(Dorling Kindersley, 1992)

*How Electricity Is Made
by C. L. Boltz (Facts on File, 1985)

I Gave Thomas Edison My Sandwich
by Floyd Moore (Albert Whitman, 1995)

The Light Bulb
by Sharon Cosner (Walker, 1984)

***The Magic School Bus and
the Electric Field Trip*** by Joanna Cole
and Bruce Degen (Scholastic, 1997)

****Quick, Annie, Give Me
a Catchy Line! A Story of
Samuel F.B. Morse***
by Robert Quackenbush
(Prentice, 1983)

Samuel Morse by Mona Kerby
(Franklin Watts, 1991)

***Samuel B. Morse: Artist
With a Message***
by John H. Tiner (Mott Media, 1987)

***They All Laughed . . .
From Light Bulbs to Lasers:
The Fascinating Stories
Behind Great Inventions
That Have Changed
Our Lives***
by Ira Flatow (HarperCollins, 1992)

****What Has Wild Tom Done Now?
A Story of Thomas Alva Edison***
by Robert Quackenbush
(Prentice, 1981)

✳ Out of print. Check your library for a circulating copy.

Software

Electric Current From the Science Court Series
Mac/Windows CD-ROM (Tom Snyder Productions). Students
learn basic concepts about electricity and do hands-on
activities to solve a "whodunit" story starring a bunch of
wisecracking cartoon characters. Includes a teacher's guide,
activity books, and a poster.

The Genius Edison Mac/Windows (The Learning
Company).This multimedia CD-ROM provides
comprehensive information about Edison and his many
inventions. Includes historic film footage, music, an interactive
time line, archival newspaper articles, and much more.

Inventor Labs Mac/Windows CD-ROM (Houghton Mifflin,
1996). This program gives students an inside look at the
virtual labs of inventors Thomas Edison, Alexander Graham Bell,
and James Watts.

Web Sites

**Invite students to meet Steve "the Dirtmeister"® Tomecek
on Scholastic Network (www.Scholasticnetwork.com/).
Steve has two sites that change regularly.**

Dirtmeister's® Science Reporters ask students to investigate,
observe, and write about the science in their world.

Hands-On Science With the Dirtmeister®
challenges students to conduct hands-on
investigations of physical phenomena.

**The following Web sites about electricity offer
historical and biographical information about inventions
and inventors, science background for teachers, and
hands-on activities.**

Electrified Ben (The Franklin Institute Science Museum)
http://sln.fi.edu/franklin/scientst/electric.html

Theater of Electricity (The Boston Museum of Science)
http://www.mos.org/sln/toe/toe.html

Thomas Edison's Home Page
http://www.thomasedison.com